# RANDAL BETZ JR.

TO MY FOUR KIDS, LUCY, RANDAL III, FINNEGAN AND BROPHY,
BE KIND TO EVERYONE, IT WILL PAY OFF, I PROMISE.

TO MY WIFE, MEGHANN, THANK YOU FOR ENCOURAGING ME TO FOLLOW
MY PASSION OF WRITING A CHILDREN'S BOOK.

TO MY CLOSE FRIEND, SCOTT EVERGNHAM, THANK YOU FOR THE WHEEL IDEA.

TO MY OTHER CLOSE FRIEND, MICHAEL WALD, THANK YOU FOR INVITING ME
TO LUNCH IN 1993, YOUR KINDNESS SPARKED THE IDEA FOR THIS BOOK.

TO THE TORTOISE BREEDER WHO GAVE ME HELIX, ANDREW HERMES,
THANK YOU FOR THE DIVINE INTERVENTION.

TO THE THREE WHO FIXED MY TERRIBLE GRAMMAR, CHRISTINE FLANAGAN,
RENEE GREENE AND JEANNE POGGI, WITHOUT TEACHERS,
THERE WOULD BE NO FUTURE.

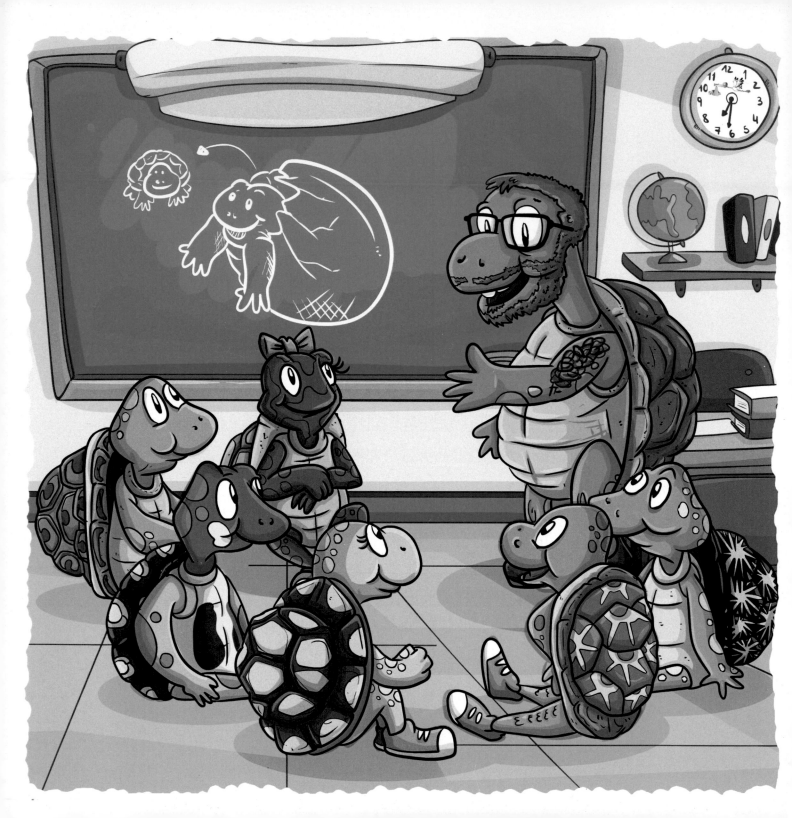

"GOOD MORNING, CLASS,"
MR. TORTY SAID.
"TODAY, WE HAVE A NEW STUDENT.
HIS NAME IS HELIX
AND HE MOVED HERE FROM FAR AWAY."

"HELIX, WOULD YOU LIKE TO TELL US
A LITTLE BIT ABOUT YOURSELF?",
MR. TORTY ASKED.
"WELL, I WAS BORN WITHOUT
BEING ABLE TO USE MY BACK LEGS,
BUT I LOVE TO HAVE FUN
AND PLAY WITH FRIENDS,"
HELIX SAID.

"HI, HELIX. MY NAME IS STAR.
WOULD YOU LIKE TO PLAY TAG WITH US?"
"I AM NOT GOOD AT TAG YET,"
HELIX SAID.
"I CAN NOT RUN FAST, BUT I WILL TRY."

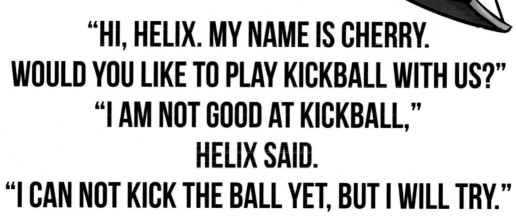

"HI, HELIX. MY NAME IS CHERRY.
WOULD YOU LIKE TO PLAY KICKBALL WITH US?"
"I AM NOT GOOD AT KICKBALL,"
HELIX SAID.
"I CAN NOT KICK THE BALL YET, BUT I WILL TRY."

"HI, HELIX. MY NAME IS SULLY.
WOULD YOU LIKE TO PLAY HOPSCOTCH WITH US?"
"I AM NOT GOOD AT HOPSCOTCH YET,"
HELIX SAID.
"I CAN NOT JUMP, BUT I WILL TRY."

"HI, HELIX. MY NAME IS PANCAKE.
WOULD YOU LIKE TO PLAY HIDE-AND-SEEK WITH US?"
"I AM NOT GOOD AT HIDE-AND-SEEK YET,"
HELIX SAID.
"I CAN NOT HIDE IN GOOD PLACES, BUT I WILL TRY."

"HI, HELIX. MY NAME IS LEO.
WOULD YOU LIKE TO PLAY FOOTBALL WITH US?"
"I AM NOT GOOD AT FOOTBALL YET,"
HELIX SAID.
"I CAN NOT RUN FAST ENOUGH TO SCORE A TOUCHDOWN,
BUT I WILL TRY."

"HI, HELIX. MY NAME IS HERMAN. I HAVE AN IDEA THAT WILL HELP YOU PLAY ALL OF THE GAMES YOU CAN'T."

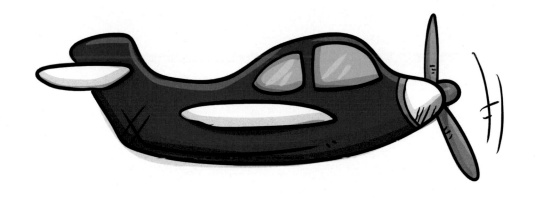

"I CAN PLAY TAG NOW!"
HELIX SAID HAPPILY.

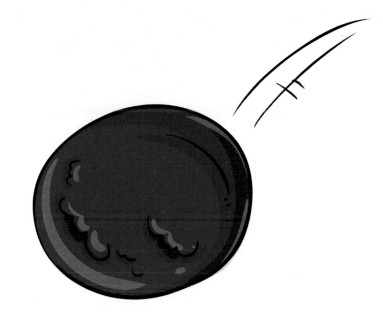

"I CAN PLAY KICKBALL NOW!"
HELIX YELLED.

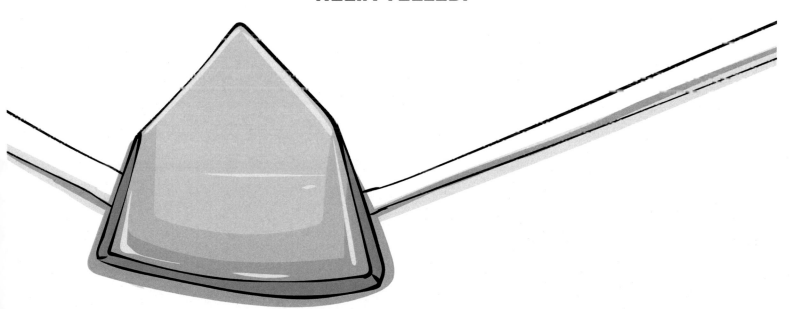

"I CAN PLAY HOPSCOTCH NOW!"
HELIX SHOUTED.

"I CAN PLAY HIDE-AND-SEEK NOW,"
HELIX WHISPERED.

"I CAN PLAY FOOTBALL NOW!"
HELIX CHEERED.

"HOW WAS YOUR FIRST DAY OF SCHOOL?"
HELIX'S MOM ASKED.
"IT WAS AWESOME AND I MADE
A LOT OF NICE FRIENDS," HELIX SAID.
"THEY HELPED ME PLAY ALL THE GAMES
I THOUGHT I WOULD NEVER BE ABLE TO PLAY."

**CHARACTER NAME: HELIX**
**COMMON NAME: MARGINATED TORTOISE**
**SCIENTIFIC NAME: TESTUDO MARGINATA**
**NATIVE HABITAT: SOUTHERN PARTS OF GREECE AND ITALY**
**DIET: HERBIVORE**
**FUN FACT: THE BLACK COLOR OF THE SHELL IS HELPFUL FOR SURVIVAL, AS IT ALLOWS THE TORTOISE TO ABSORB A GREAT DEAL OF HEAT IN A SHORT TIME, HELPING IT MAINTAIN ITS BODY TEMPERATURE.**

**CHARACTER NAME: STAR**
**COMMON NAME: INDIAN STAR TORTOISE**
**SCIENTIFIC NAME: GEOCHELONE ELEGANS**
**NATIVE HABITAT: INDIA, PAKISTAN AND SRI LANKA.**
**DIET: HERBIVORE**

**FUN FACT: THE INDIAN STAR TORTOISE HAS A BLACK SHELL WITH YELLOW, STAR-SHAPED MARKINGS WHICH PROVIDE CAMOUFLAGE WITH ITS NATURAL SURROUNDINGS.**

**CHARACTER NAME: CHERRY**
**COMMON NAME: CHERRY-HEAD RED-FOOTED TORTOISE**
**SCIENTIFIC NAME: CHELONOIDIS CARBONARIA**
**NATIVE HABITAT: CENTRAL AND SOUTH AMERICA**
**DIET: OMNIVORE**

**FUN FACT: JUVENILE RED-FOOTED TORTOISES MAKE CLUCK OR CHIRP LIKE NOISES WHILE FORAGING FOR FOOD**

**CHARACTER NAME: SULLY**
COMMON NAME: **SULCATA TORTOISE**
SCIENTIFIC NAME: **CENTROCHELYS SULCATA**
NATIVE HABITAT: **AFRICA**
DIET: **HERBIVORE**
FUN FACT: **THE SULCATA TORTOISE IS THE THIRD LARGEST SPECIES OF TORTOISE IN THE WORLD. THE GALAPAGOS TORTOISE SPECIES ARE THE LARGEST AND THE ALDABRA TORTOISE SPECIES ARE THE SECOND LARGEST.**

**CHARACTER NAME: PANCAKE**
**COMMON NAME: PANCAKE TORTOISE**
**SCIENTIFIC NAME: MALACOCHERSUS TORNIERI**
**NATIVE HABITAT: EAST AFRICA**
**DIET: HERBIVORE**

**FUN FACT:** WHEN HIDING FROM PREDATORS, THEY WILL WEDGE THEMSELVES INTO TINY GAPS IN THE ROCKS AND PUFF UP THEIR BODY TO MAKE IT VERY DIFFICULT TO BE PULLED OUT.

CHARACTER NAME: **LEO**
COMMON NAME: **LEOPARD TORTOISE**
SCIENTIFIC NAME: **STIGMOCHELYS PARDALIS**
NATIVE HABITAT: **AFRICA**
DIET: **HERBIVORE**
FUN FACT: **NO TWO LEOPARD TORTOISES HAVE THE SAME SHELL PATTERN.**

# HELIX

HELIX IS A MARGINATED TORTOISE WHO HATCHED ON JULY 31ST, 2019 IN WITTMAN, ARIZONA. HE WAS BORN WITH A CONGENITAL SPINAL DISORDER, PREVENTING HIM FROM USING HIS BACK LEGS. IN FACT, HIS BACK LEGS STUCK STRAIGHT UP IN THE AIR, SO HE COULD NOT USE THEM AT ALL. HELIX WAS FLOWN OVERNIGHT TO WILMINGTON, DELAWARE. HIS FIRST FEW DAYS HE PROVED THAT HE WAS NOT GOING TO LET HIS PHYSICAL CHALLENGE GET IN THE WAY OF BEING A TORTOISE. HELIX WAS DETERMINED TO LIVE HIS LIFE, JUST LIKE ALL THE OTHER TORTOISES. HELIX GOT XRAYS AND A CT SCAN, WHICH SHOWED HE IN FACT HAD A SPINAL DEFORMITY. IT ALSO SHOWED THAT HE HAD A SIGNIFICANTLY SMALLER RIGHT LUNG. HE HAD A HARD TIME GETTING AROUND, SO HE WAS FITTED WITH SOME VERY SMALL SKATEBOARD WHEELS. FROM THAT MOMENT ON, HELIX HAS BEEN UNSTOPPABLE. HIS GRIT TO ALWAYS MOVE FORWARD IS INSPIRATIONAL. LET HELIX INSPIRE YOU TO NEVER GIVE UP AND TO REMIND YOU THAT IT IS OKAY TO SLOW DOWN, AS LONG YOU CONTINUE TO MOVE FORWARD.

FOLLOW HELIX ON FACEBOOK AND INSTAGRAM (@HELIXWHEELS) FOR DAILY UPDATES.